Legacy Planning

Take Control of Your Future

Get the Protection You and Your Family Deserve

Achieve peace of mind and be shielded from creditors and predators

ENSURE YOUR LEGACY

Call our office today:
(435)218-7773

<u>www.saintgeorgelaw.com/legacybook</u>

Make your appointment for a
FREE 30-MINUTE CONSULTATION
(A $300 value)

Our holistic approach will see you through from start to finish

DISCLAIMER PAGE

Copyright © 2018 by Travis R. Christiansen

All rights reserved. No part of this book may be used or reproduced in any manner whatsoever without prior written consent of the author, except as provided by the United States of America copyright law.

Published 2018
Printed in the United States of America.

ISBN 9781731247636

Additional copies are available at special quantity discounts for bulk purchases for sales promotions, premiums, fundraising, and educational use.
For more information, please contact:

Travis R. Christiansen

The Publisher and Author make no representations or warranties with respect to the accuracy or completeness of the contents of this work and specifically disclaim all warranties, including without limitation warranties of fitness for a particular purpose. No warranty may be created or extended by sales or promotional materials. The advice and strategies contained herein may not be suitable for every situation. This work is sold with the understanding that the publisher is not engaged in rendering legal, account or other professional services. If professional assistance is required, the services of a competent professional person should be sought. Neither the Publisher nor the Author shall be liable for damages arising here from. The fact that an organization or website is referred to in this work as a citation and/or potential source of further information does not mean the that Author or Publisher endorses the information the organization or website may provide or recommendations it may make. Further, readers should be aware that the internet websites listed in this work may have changed or disappeared between when this work was written and when it was read.

Table of Contents

[INTRODUCTION .... 5](#)

[WELCOME TO MY BOOK! .... 5](#)

[CHAPTER 1 .... 9](#)

[NIGHTMARE MISTAKES .... 9](#)

[CHAPTER 2 .... 16](#)

[JUST WHAT IN THE WORLD IS ESTATE PLANNING? .... 16](#)

[CHAPTER 3 .... 19](#)

[WHY IS ESTATE PLANNING NECESSARY? .... 20](#)

[CHAPTER 4 .... 25](#)

[WHAT DOCUMENTS DO I NEED TO PREPARE? .... 25](#)

[CHAPTER 5 .... 28](#)

[IS IT REALLY NECESSARY? .... 28](#)

[CHAPTER 6 .... 34](#)

[WHAT IS PROBATE AND WHY IS IT BAD? .... 34](#)

[CHAPTER 7 .... 37](#)

INTESTACY, OR, WHAT THE GOVERNMENT SAYS. 37

CHAPTER 8 39

WHAT ARE MY OPTIONS? 39

CHAPTER 9 55

WHEN DO YOU NEED TO SEE YOUR ATTORNEY AGAIN? 55

CHAPTER 10 58

CHOOSING AN ESTATE PLANNING ATTORNEY 58

(AND WHY TO CHOOSE ME) 58

CHAPTER 11 60

FINAL CONSIDERATION FOR THOSE WITH MINOR CHILDREN 60

CHAPTER 12 62

WHY SHOULD I WORK WITH YOUR ESTATE PLANNING TEAM? 62

Introduction

Welcome to my book!

First off because I am an attorney, I should make a disclaimer that this book is not intended to be specific legal advice for any individual or family's situation.

It is meant to be an educational offering to assist you in beginning the process of estate planning. I have done my best to ensure the legal accuracy of any statements made in this book. However, please know that between state and federal legislative, as well as court action, the law is in a constant state of change and any information given in this book should be taken as general in nature.

Also, because the law changes constantly you should consult with an attorney prior to beginning any estate planning process.

Estate planning is most simply defined as stating your wishes as to what should be done after your passing. Estate planning is necessary to provide for guardianship of any minor children, as well as to provide an efficient distribution and management of any assets.

In this book I will attempt to demonstrate through real-life experiences situations where people have done things right and where improvements could have been made. It is my hope that by reviewing this book you will see some of the benefits of estate planning for you and your family, and why regular reviews are important.

It is said we should see our doctor annually to check up on our physical health. We should see the dentist every six months. We see our accountant every year about our taxes. However, many people do not realize that estate plans need to be reviewed at least annually by you and your attorney.

This is especially true if there are any significant changes in your family or circumstances. Some of these changes could include the death of a child or spouse, remarriage, becoming empty nesters, or inheriting a large sum of money yourself. These are just some examples of the many things that may create a need to make changes or updates to your plan

I strongly encourage and recommend that you schedule a short review with me or your attorney on an annual basis. This is to ensure everything is as it should be, and that the individuals chosen to manage your affairs after your passing are still able and willing to do so.

This book will walk through some of the mistakes that many people make and some of the tragedies that have occurred because of these mistakes.

We will examine various estate planning vehicles and choices, and I will describe the process that a competent attorney will go through in preparing an estate plan. Because of changes in the law, there are some aspects of an estate plan that may benefit you while you are living that did not exist before.

I thank you for taking the time to read this short book, and I hope that it will be of benefit to you and your family. You can schedule a free consultation by contacting my firm through our website at www.saintgeorgelaw.com. You can also call us at 435-218-7773 to schedule a complementary consultation.

I wrote this book because I'm passionate about helping people gain control over their lives and achieve their good work on Earth. I sincerely hope you enjoy these insights. If you need more specific and personal help, please skip ahead to the end to learn how to get a free consultation (normally valued at $300), so we can strategize together about how to reach your goals in a way that resonates with your priorities and values.

Thank you

Travis R. Christiansen

Chapter 1

Nightmare Mistakes

Joint Tenancy

Imagine, if you will, you have been in your home for 40 years. This is the home in which you raised your children. You cried, laughed, mourned, and celebrated your lives with your family in this home.

One day you return from your usual days errands to find that a Notice of Sheriff's Sale of your home has been posted by the attorney of a former son-in-law.

One of your daughter's, despite your best efforts, has had struggles with addiction.

In her divorce, her ex-husband has been awarded a judgment against her for unpaid debt and child support. Some time ago, in order to avoid the cost of probate or setting up an estate plan, you heard that if you listed your child as a joint tenant with rights of survivorship on your home when you and your spouse passed away, they would inherit your home automatically. You are a good loving parent and wanted to make sure that your daughter kept the family home. Therefore, she followed this advice, and she now owns 1/3 of your home.

It was good idea. It was frugal. But now you find yourself with approximately 30 days to either sell your home or obtain the means to pay off this judgment from unpaid child support.

This is exactly what happened to the parents of one of my divorce clients. In the end, they ended up having to sell their home for only about 80% of its value in order to satisfy the ex-husband of their daughter. In an effort to save a few thousand dollars these good, loving parents ended up losing much more.

They lost potential sale value of their home in excess of $30,000 and they had to pay a $15,000 judgment on behalf of their daughter. They were forced to move from their home of more than forty years in their mid-70s, under a thirty-day time crunch.

I used to think that this was only a law school hypothetical and it was one that I certainly used in talking with clients about estate planning. However, seeing these good people go through this was gut-wrenching for me.

This is one of the main objectives in writing this. My hope in gaining a wide audience in an effort to encourage more people to tend to their estate planning and avoid this very circumstance.

Failure to Review and Update

Once you have an estate plan in place it is essential that you sit down with your attorney at least annually to review it and keep it current. It is also critical to meet with your attorney after a major life event that may affect your plan. Consider the following example:

The facts are essentially this: two sisters who had never married lived together, worked together and shared a home. They had both established trusts wherein upon the death of the first sister the remaining part that sister's interest in the home would pass to the other sister.

However, after the first sister passed away the second sister failed follow-up with the attorney to have her estate plan updated.

When she passed away, the firm I was working for was retained to administer her estate. Because she had not been diligent in updating her estate it was necessary for us to identify, track down, and give proper legal notice to, if I remember correctly, fifty-six people; many of whom were second cousins who she had never met or had not seen in several decades.

I should add that all of this happened in the days before Google and Facebook the search was difficult. It required the retention of private investigators and other means to track these people down. After all of this, when the home was sold, each of these 56 people received a check for their equal share of the estate -- less than $100.00.

I don't know if the surviving sister was just busy with life and hadn't taken the time or felt the need to review her estate plan with her attorney. It may have been that she was hesitant to pay the couple hundred dollars to have her attorney review her estate plan with her attorney. Or, she may have mistakenly believed that the planning was already done. Needless to say, a small fortune was spent after she had passed to give a pittance to her remaining fifty-six heirs.

Top Secret Plan

I am currently involved in a probate case that is going to be more complicated than it needs to be. I represent the sister of a deceased man who was very careful and most likely has a will or some other plan in place. However, that estate plan is likely in one of several safes in his home. He and He alone had the combinations. We are initially proceeding under intestacy (without a will) and may find that we need to make an amendment to the probate if we discover a plan once we get the legal authority to open the safes.

Give your family a copy of your estate plan. Give them copies of any amendments and updates. Make sure they know where the originals are kept and have access to them!

Failure to Fund

One last common mistake is a failure to fund the trust. A trust is useless unless it is funded! At the very lease you need to move your real property and bank accounts to the trust. Almost every defect of a trust can be fixed except the lack of properly funding the trust.

I should add that years ago I would trust some clients to do this on their own. Now, I will, at a minimum, record the deed to their home for them. I have considered increasing my fees and driving my clients to the bank to move their bank accounts as well

Have I got your attention? I hope so! My goal is to convince you to do two things:

1. **Get an estate plan done by an attorney after a thorough consultation, and**
2. **Make sure you have annual reviews with that attorney!**

Chapter 2

Just What in the World is Estate Planning?

The most basic definition of estate planning is the putting in place of a plan for the disposition of your assets after you have passed. However, well-thought-out estate planning involves working with an estate planning attorney, a tax advisor, a financial professional, and others who might be involved given your specific circumstance.

The process of planning your estate will typically begin with an initial consultation with an attorney. In this meeting you are likely to discuss, in approximate terms, your net worth and estate planning goals.

If you are comfortable with the attorney you will then schedule a follow-up meeting with either the attorney or his or her paralegal to get a more detailed description of your assets, debts, and distribution plan ideas.

After the law firm has this information, they may contact your CPA or tax advisor and/or your financial advisor to make sure that the goals that you have discussed with these other professionals are in line with the goals expressed to the attorney.

Once the attorney has gathered all of this information, they will typically go to their inventory of estate planning tools and propose one or two ideas to you to successfully execute your wishes.

It is very helpful at this point, if your attorney is familiar with various financial instruments such as annuities, variable annuities, life insurance, mutual funds, 401(k)s, IRAs, etc. An attorney who is not familiar with these may very well set up estate planning documents that do not work cohesively with your financial accounts.

This is one of the reasons that I personally became life insurance licensed. I also hold several securities designations. I understand the power of many of these financial instruments.

If the plan makes sense then the attorney and his staff will work to create the plan documents and schedule a time for you to come in and review them. At this time, it would be wise to take the time to review the documents, especially checking for spellings of various family names.

If the documents are all in order, and the necessary people are available, you may be able to sign them in this appointment. However, if your plan is complex requiring multiple documents you may want to take your documents home and review them with family members prior to execution.

A thorough estate planning process in which the most basic documents are used should cost at least $1000.00. Any less and you have not hired an attorney, nor paid for legal advice. You've merely hired a document drafter who is looking to turn a quick buck on a simple document.

A more complex estate plan can run into the tens of thousands of dollars depending on your goals, tax situation, and the size of your estate. On average a good estate plan will run from $2,000.00 to $10,000.00

Chapter 3

Why is Estate Planning Necessary?

The short answer is to avoid probate. Other purposes can include tax planning and seeing that the needs of minor children are taking care of should you die young.

Another reason to make sure that estate planning is done is to avoid many of the problems that I've discussed in prior sections of this book. Most, if not all, of the worst-case scenarios mentioned above could have been prevented had these individuals contacted an attorney before they took the actions they took.

When a person has minor children, it is tantamount that they have at the very least a will. Otherwise, it will be up to a judge to determine who raises their children in the unfortunate event that they pass away before their children are raised.

I have seen this result in protracted battles between family members. In other cases, I have seen the heart-breaking circumstance of no one stepping forward, and being willing to raise the children.

In my area we are blessed with excellent judges. However, they may not choose a family member to raise the children whose values are similar to those of the parents. Therefore, if you would like a say in which family member or friend raises your children, you should see an attorney and at the very least create a will.

Another reason for estate planning is to smooth the transition and transfer of assets after your passing. From the examples given above, if assets are not dealt with through an estate plan, there can be great expense and difficulty in getting those assets to the persons you desire.

Whether you're an "invincible" healthy young woman in her mid-20's or a 50-something-year-old entrepreneur on your third big venture, you probably don't relish the thought of taking time out of your busy life to contemplate what will happen to you when you become unwell and when you die.

This is normal – it's human nature to want to avoid these kinds of conversations.

That said, since you're reading this book, you already understand (to a degree) that you need such plans in place. However, you may not fully appreciate the full purpose of estate planning.

Here's a prospective you might not have considered. The late General (and President) Dwight D. Eisenhower once offered the following Yoda-like observation: "plans are useless, but planning is indispensable."

What Eisenhower meant by that strange statement is that the plans you make today – before you go to battle or get sick – will change as circumstances change. You can never figure out what an enemy will do in a war or how new tax laws will evolve or how the stock market will flow.

However, the act of planning *in and of itself* organizes you to meet the surprises of the future more nimbly.

Holly had a solid estate plan that reflected her priorities. She got sick with leukemia and had to spend months in the hospital. But she managed her business and finances because she had done the spadework when she was well.

The farm analogy rings true. You sew the field in good weather, so you can reap the harvest and eat in bad weather.

Preparation helps your family. Rodrigo suddenly died in a car accident, leaving his two small children and spouse faced with possible bills, creditors and tax headaches. Although grieving, his family was relieved that he had done his due diligence, obtained the right insurance and established trusts, Rodrigo shielded his loved ones from creditors, helped his estate bypass problematic taxation and gave his wife money (through the insurance) to raise the family.

Knowing that your plans are solid lets you be more carefree and spontaneous. Form follows function. It's a lot easier (and less scary) to cross a bridge across a chasm when there's a sturdy railing.

Chapter 4

What Documents do I Need to Prepare?

An estate plan does not have to be complicated. Consider, for example, the case of a single working mother who wants to keep her estate plan simple. As a working mom, Amanda, didn't have a lot of time to mull a deep investment strategy or do anything fancy. Plus didn't have a lot in savings.

Her aim was to get the "minimum done" before her third child was born and then figure out a more detailed strategy later, when she had breathing room.

I might tell Amanda to create the following documents:

- **Advanced healthcare directive**. She would provide written guidance for Eric (and for her doctors) about what to do if she became incapacitated and what treatments she would like.

- **Durable power of attorney.** This document would allow Eric (or another trusted person) to make legal decisions for her, if she became incapacitated.

- **HIPAA release form.** HIPAA is a law designed to protect the privacy of patients. It can be a double-edged sword, since it can prevent people like Eric or Amanda's mother from accessing her medical records and treatment information without having to go through an elaborate process. The HIPAA release bypasses that mess.

- **Will or revocable living trust.** This document determines how Amanda wants her assets allocated after she dies and provides instructions for her heirs. Amanda might also want to include a document detailing what she wants done with her computer files and popular blog as well.

With that basic preparation done, she can feel more secure, although she'd likely benefit from a more detailed strategy and a regular reassessment of her financial world and priorities.

Chapter 5

Is it Really Necessary?

I am often asked if estate planning is necessary. Some will say "I just don't have any money." However, estate planning can be important and can help people in any income or wealth bracket.

Consider the following example

> Charles' sister Nancy, was on the autism spectrum. Their father (the last surviving parent) died without putting together an estate plan. Nancy had lived at home with the father; she had no job or connections in the neighborhood because of her disability.
>
> The father had run a small retail business that wasn't worth much when he died. But he bought his home back in the 1960s, and the property was now worth $1.2 million. Charles's

plan was to sell the home and split the proceeds between him and Nancy. But there was a big problem. If Nancy inherited these assets, she would become ineligible to collect Social Security Income (SSI) benefits. She needed that money to pay for things like clothes, groceries, medical needs, etc.

Charles fixed the problem by establishing a first party special needs trust to serve as a trustee. Nancy would continue to receive SSI (as long as Charles remained alive), and the trust could purchase important things for her, such as a television or trip to the Bahamas.

Of course, had Nancy's father established a special needs trust back when he was alive; Charles would not have had to go through this song and dance.

The moral here is: planning is a "must-do" project, not a "would like to do if I have the time one day" project.

What will it cost if I delay or do not do any estate planning?

The costs in terms of money, time and peace of mind could be huge.

But shockingly, 55% of Americans die without estate plans. Why is that?

To answer that, let's turn to bestselling author, Stephen Covey ("The 7 Habits of Highly Effective People"), a book I have read several times, who built a quadrant model to discuss how people prioritize things. Per Covey:

- **Quadrant 1 activities are urgent and important**, such as paying your taxes when they are due. We get them done.

- **Quadrant 3 activities are urgent but not important,** such as watching a football game on Sunday night. We tend to respond to the "latest and loudest," so most people do a lot of Quadrant 1 and 3 things.

- **Quadrant 4 concerns activities that are neither important, nor urgent**, such as playing Candy Crush online. Most of us spend far too much time in Quadrant 4 than we'd like to admit!

- **Quadrant 2 is unique. It concerns *important* activities that are not urgent.** Estate planning falls squarely in Quadrant 2.

The more time and energy we devote to Quadrant 2 activities, the richer and better our lives and legacies become. But, working in Quadrant 2 requires focus as well as a deep appreciation of what really matters in life.

Keep that in mind as we go through the following example.

Consider the case of Rosaline. After her sister died, she hired an estate planning lawyer to handle the estate. Rosaline was 64, and her sister, Carolyn, was 75 when she died. Carolyn had a will, not a trust, forcing the estate to be probated.

Rosaline saw the cumbersome probate process for what it was, but she refused to get her own estate plan in order. In fact, she spent *11 years* avoiding the work. Why? Because she was estranged from her son, who had left the house when he was a teenager and who had avoided contact with his mother ever since.

As Rosaline approached retirement age, she launched a quest to find and reconnect with her son – who, at this point, was in his 50s. But he still refused to see her. And since he was only her child, Rosaline abandoned the idea of planning. When she finally passed away, her younger brother, Avis, contacted the same estate planning attorney who worked on Carolyn's estate long ago.

They both assumed Rosaline's estate would be modest, but it turned out to be worth over $1.4 million. However, probate costs, legal fees and taxes stripped Rosaline's estate of much of its value – money that could have been earmarked for a good cause, like a charity or her younger brother's children's education.

Estate planning is not just about *your* comfort level and needs. It's also about your *legacy* – about your family, your friends, the causes you believe in, the good work you do on earth.

When you fail to plan, you don't just hurt yourself, you also, in effect, turn your back on those who need your help.

Should you choose not to create an estate plan, your state legislature has created an estate plan for you. And we all know that our elected officials always have our best interest at heart. We will talk about this process in a later chapter.

Chapter 6

What is Probate and why is it Bad?

In short *probate* is the process of transferring the assets of someone who is passed away to those who would be entitled to receive them under the law. Probate is done through the courts, and can either be formal or informal.

Informal probate is when the personal representative designated under the will carries out the terms of the will without extensive court supervision. They do this unless an heir feels that they are not following the provisions of the will and decides to take the matter to court.

Formal probate is very closely supervised by the courts. Regular reports need to be made to the courts, and at times approval of actions brought before the court prior to the action being taken.

As discussed, probate can be a lengthy and costly process and proper estate planning can greatly benefit people in handling this process or avoiding it all together.

Some states permit probate through what is sometimes referred to as a small estate affidavit. In this process, the designated personal representative signs an affidavit, or sworn statement on a state approved form indicating that the person who is passed away had a small estate as defined by the law.

This will allow some assets to be transferred without probate. I recently had a client successfully use this to recover some money from a bank account owned by her husband that she did not know about when he died.

However, you should keep in mind that real estate generally must be probated unless it is planned for through a trust.

Some assets can pass without probate, such as a pay on death bank account, or through a beneficiary designation on an IRA, annuity, or life insurance policy.

Chapter 7

Intestacy, or, What the Government Says.

What happens if you were to pass away without having planned your estate? The answer to that is intestacy.

Intestacy is the process that the state legislature has said should happen to your accumulated assets if you die without a plan. They have used their collective judgment as to what would be the most fair or best way to distribute someone's estate. Unfortunately, this is a one-size-fits-all solution and too often we fall into this process due to a lack of prior planning.

I have had to litigate intestacy on several occasions. This is especially difficult in a second marriage situation.

Sometimes the surviving spouse is entitled to all or most of the estate. A person's children, from a previous marriage would then get little, if any, of the estate. This may definitely not be what the deceased would have wanted.

If you have any assets at all, intestacy should be avoided at all costs. The biggest fights in these tend to be people trying to assert a claim such as – "mom said I could have this" – or – "dad said I could have that."

One of the surviving children will try to be the leader in the family. It often creates enormous conflict within the family, as they try and sort through their parent's assets and follow the law.

It never ceases to amaze me the effect that a sudden windfall or the potential for a sudden windfall can have on people and families.

A well thought out and executed estate plan can have a tremendous amount of influence on family harmony.

Chapter 8

What are My Options?

What is a Will?

A will is the document by which you state what you want to happen to your assets when you die. You can also set out your preference for a guardian of your minor children upon your death.

There are several different types of wills. While I will discuss some of them, this is not an exhaustive or complete list by any means. It will, however, give you an idea of the basic types of wills.

The first type is a *holographic will*. This is a will that is written in a person's own handwriting (it cannot be typed) and witnessed in accordance to law.

Holographic wills are just as effective as any other will. However, they may miss important parts that a good estate planning attorney would include in a will. Holographic wills are not as common as they once were, because the courts have set pretty strict rules about how they can work.

The next type of will is what I call a *simple will*. This is a fairly basic document prepared by an attorney that basically says two things: (1) when I die do this with my property and (2) if I have any kids this is who I would like to raise them and take care of them.

Another type of will that was popular many years ago but is not as popular at the present time is what estate planning attorneys would call a *testamentary trust*.

This is basically a will, that by its function, establishes a trust. My opinion is that several years ago estate planning attorneys used this is a business continuation model. They would prepare the will that names them as the trustee or one of the trustees of the testamentary trust.

When a client passed away, they would begin to get additional work by functioning as a trustee. These have largely fallen out of favor and are not used very often any more, although they do have their place

The most common type in my practice is what is referred to as a *pour over will*. This is a will that is prepared as part of a comprehensive estate planning package. It serves as a safety net and provides that any property that was not put into a person's trust will be put into their trust upon their death.

These are always a good idea, and I've had to rely on them in several cases recently. Most recently I had a situation where someone had refinanced a home. It had been placed in their trust as part of their estate planning work. As part of that refinance the title company at the insistence of their mortgage holder transferred title to their home from the trust to their individual names.

However, they had not transferred the home back into the trust after the refinance. We had to do a probate to put the asset back in the trust for distribution. This whole process ended up costing my client more than $3,000.00 and resulted in months of delays.

What is a trust and who are the people involved in a trust?

A trust is where someone places property in trust for the benefit of someone. The beneficiary can be the person who created the trust. The property is held by a trustee for the beneficiary at the direction of the trustor. These different people are described below.

The first person in a trust is known by many names. The person who creates a trust can be referred to as the *grantor, trustor, or settlor*. This is the person who will typically transfer property into a trust and sets the terms and conditions of the trust.

The second person is the *trustee*. There can be more than one trustee. The trustee's job is to manage the property placed in the trust by the trustor in accordance with the terms set out in the trust.

Trustees have a fiduciary duty to act in accordance with the trust, and in the best interest of the beneficiaries. There are two types of trustees. Typically, there is an initial trustee or trustees and successor trustee or trustees. The initial trustee(s) are immediately in power over the trust. Successor trustees take over when the initial trustees are no longer able or willing to function.

Some types of trusts require that various trustees have different roles. You might have a management trustee and an investment trustee. The management trustee manages and runs the assets and the investment trustee sees to the investments of the trust and makes those decisions separate from the other trustees.

This brings us to the next person in the trust of which there are two classifications: *Beneficiaries*.

The first is what we would call a life or initial beneficiary. This person is entitled to the income and use of the assets of the trust in accordance with the trust. Their use is subject to the powers and control of the trustee during their lifetime.

The second type of beneficiary is often referred to as a remainder beneficiary. The remainder beneficiary gets what is left over, or the remainder of the trust, usually after the death of the life beneficiary

Another person that can be involved in a trust is referred to as a *trust protector*. The trust protector's job is essentially to oversee the trustee. They are given the ability to remove the trustee if the trustee is not following the directions of the trust or acting in the best interest of the beneficiaries.

The most common type of trust is typically called a *family living trust*. This is very often a revocable document. The initial trustor, trustee and income or life beneficiary are usually the same people.

Essentially a couple will create a trust in which they appoint themselves as the trustee and name themselves as the initial beneficiaries. They will then name successor trustees to take over management of the assets in the event of their incapacity or death, and persons to receive the income and assets of the trust after their passing.

There are a lot of different types of trust other than a simple living or family trust. I am going to give some basic information about some of the more common specialized types of trusts:

Credit Shelter or A/B Trusts

These were a very common type of trust before the estate tax laws began to change dramatically in 2001 and again in late 2017. Since then, they have not been as common. There are some pitfalls to these trusts and they should be used carefully.

They are used to essentially double the amount of assets that can be passed to a couple's heirs without an estate tax being paid.

My firm has recently seen some issues with old A/B trusts that are now causing some difficulties for clients. There are solutions, but they need to be addressed before one of the spouses passes away. If you have an old Credit Shelter or A/B trust please get it reviewed and updated if necessary.

Charitable Trusts

A charitable trust is just what it sounds like. It is a trust that has some component of a charitable gift. There are two basic types of charitable trusts.

The first and most common is a charitable remainder trust (CRT). A CRT has two forms, a charitable remainder annuity trust (CRAT) and a charitable remainder unitrust (CRUT). A CRAT is where you use a lump sum of money to purchase an annuity from which you intend to take the income. Any money left in the trust upon your death goes to the charity you have designated. A CRUT is where you hold some asset that is not an annuity.

The second type of charitable trust is a charitable lead trust. In this instance the charity gets the income during your lifetime and then your heirs (usually family) get the remainder.

I am a fan of charitable giving. However, a charitable trust, should be done in consultation with your tax professional and financial advisor. There are some amazing financial tools that can make doing this particularly easy in many instances.

Special Needs Trusts

Special needs trusts are designed to allow individuals with special needs to qualify or maintain "needs-based" government benefits such as Medicaid and supplemental security income.

In general, eligibility for these programs requires that a disabled recipient have less than $2000.00 "countable assets" and limited income. When properly designed, assets held in special needs trust will not be considered "countable" for Medicaid and SSI eligibility.

However, those assets held in the trust can still be used to supplement needs-based government benefits and provide many of the good things in life such as electronics, companionship, vacations, hair care, dental, education, etc.

In order to qualify for need-based government programs the individual need to be over the age of 65, blind, or disabled. To be considered disabled for purposes of Medicaid and SSI, a person must be unable to: "engage in any substantial gainful activity by reason of a medically determinable physical or mental impairment, which can be expected to result in death, or which has lasted or can be expected to last for continuous period of not less than 12 months" (20 CFR section 416.905).

There are two tests that are used to determine whether someone may qualify for Medicaid or SSI, they are an income test and an asset test. The numbers and qualifications under both of these tests change periodically, so I won't include those criteria in this book.

Needless to say, it is currently an asset base of less than $2,000.00 with the exception of household goods, tools used for work, a certain amount of home-equity, funds set aside for a funeral, and personal effects.

In the income test disabled individuals cannot make more than $1,170.00 a month and blind individuals cannot make more than $1,950.00 per month. Eligibility for Medicaid and SSI does vary from state to state.

Asset Protection Trusts

These are a relatively new development and they are statutory. Some states offer these; some states do not. The requirements vary from state to state and I'm speaking only of Utah when I describe the asset protection trust concept.

A domestic protection trust is one in which a person or persons place assets in an irrevocable trust that meets the specific requirements of Utah law. Some of those requirements are that the grantor or creator of the trust has limited power over the trust after it is created. Often this trust will have more than one trustee.

Who should Consider Setting up a Utah Asset Protection Trust(UDAPT)?
You should consider a UDAPT if you are in a high-liability profession, or if you have a high net worth. It is also a good option if

you just want to shield some of your hard-earned assets from creditors such as a home, investment accounts, a business, a cabin, a ranch, or other real estate from creditors.

UDAPTs are frequently used to protect a nest-egg. They help to ensure that you have enough assets protected to live a comfortable life, especially given the litigious and unpredictable world we live in where lawsuits can be brought against you for any reason or no reason at all.

How does a UDAPT Work?

Under Utah's asset protection trust laws, you are allowed to fund a trust with any type of assets you want to protect. You maintain complete control over the investment of the assets in the trust, and you can name yourself, your spouse, and your family as beneficiaries of the trust to receive the assets if you need them in the future, so long as you have a co-trustee who makes distribution decisions. The statute does not prevent you from naming a trusted friend, family member, or advisor as the co-trustee.

For the trust to be effective in shielding your assets against creditors, the trust must have at least one Utah trustee, it must hold some Utah assets (but it can also hold assets in other states), and you must sign an affidavit declaring that you are still solvent (meaning you have more assets than liabilities) after making any contribution to the trust.

The trust must be irrevocable, but flexibility can be built into the trust to allow for the removal and replacement of trustees and to change the ultimate distribution of the assets upon your death. Once you have appropriately moved assets into your UDAPT, those assets are immediately protected against future involuntary creditors.

Existing creditors are limited to bringing a fraudulent conveyance claim within the later of two years after the property is transferred to the trust, or one year after the creditor reasonably could have discovered the transfer. This period can be reduced to 120 days by sending notice to known creditors, and by publishing notice for unknown creditors.

Often, it is good to establish a trust protector to assist in the management and oversight of trustees other than yourself.

Family Partnerships

It used to be a fairly common practice in estate planning to create a family limited partnership. A family limited partnership is when the mother and father establish a limited partnership. They would be the general partners and they would name their children as limited partners. It is designed to take advantage of the annual gift tax exclusion and gradually gift, over a period of years, the ownership of an asset to their children without ever giving up control.

This was a common practice with family farms and real estate. If the value of the asset was such that it would cause an estate tax problem, we would take advantage of the annual gift tax exclusion and gradually transfer the illiquid asset to the children as limited partners. This would minimize the taxable estate and avoid the need to fire sell or encumber the asset to pay the estate tax.

Since the United States Congress has substantially increased the exemption amounts from the estate tax these are a less common vehicle. However, there may be an old family limited partnership that was set up perhaps by your parents or grandparents, that might be worth reviewing with an attorney to see if there would be a more efficient means of distributing the asset at this time.

Chapter 9

When do you need to see your attorney again?

Congratulations! You have an estate plan. You are done. You have a nice, new, shiny binder full of paperwork that you may or may not understand. You, or your attorney, have sent deeds off to the various County recorders' office to change title. You have even gone down to the bank and changed your bank accounts into the name of the trust, or other estate planning vehicle that you may have set up. So now what?

It is my strongest recommendation that you sit down and review your estate plan with your estate planning attorney at least

annually. You should also meet with your estate planning attorney whenever there has been a substantial change in the circumstances of your life such as death or adoption of a child, the death of a spouse, the acquisition of new significant assets, or the desire to divest yourself of assets or change assets classification such as liquidating a home to purchase an RV.
You should also review your estate plan if your planning was done while you still had minor children. Perhaps you should amend and name one of your children as successor trustee.

If there has been a significant change in the lives of one of your children you should review your plan. Many times, a child develops difficulties, such as addiction, divorce, or bankruptcy that may require some adjustments to your estate plan. This will prevent your assets from being wasted or seized by being given outright to that particular child out of the trust upon your death.

One of the most expensive and difficult things for many people is not having reviewed their estate plan on a regular basis.

After one spouse passes away and there have been substantial changes, it can be time consuming and expensive to restore things to the original intent of the plan. It may involve the costs and delays of probate. Many of these expenses can be avoided with regular plan reviews and updates.

I know of some law firms that regularly charge their clients an annual maintenance fee by getting approval ahead of time to charge their credit card on the anniversary of the estate plan creation. I will be glad to do this if you would like. This is a good reminder to come in and review your estate plan and any significant changes in your life. I would be happy to set this up for you.

Chapter 10

Choosing an Estate Planning Attorney

(And why to choose me)

There are a lot of other issues other than just the estate planning documents that may need to be considered in creating your estate plan. These could include debt you are carrying, the makeup of your assets - particularly investment accounts, and retirement accounts. You may also have potential tax issues to consider.

One thing that I think sets our office apart is that I have been life insurance and securities licensed for almost as long as I have been practicing law. This gives me a unique perspective on estate planning. Sometimes there may be a financial tool that would accomplish your estate planning goals in a way that would minimize what you have to pay out-of-pocket.

As an example, I have a client who has a net worth in excess of $2 million. We were able to take $1.8 million of this money and, using financial products, distribute this to her grandkids without the need of any estate planning documents and with no out-of-pocket costs to her.

Another reason that I think I merit consideration as an effective estate planning attorney is that I have seen the inside of a courtroom. I have litigated trusts and the application of various trust language. I have had to do probates of people who had done no planning and have seen the devastation and family problems it can cause. For these reasons I'm passionate about estate planning and seek to help and do the best job I can for my clients.

Chapter 11

Final Consideration for Those with Minor Children

One of the principal purposes of estate planning for those with minor children, is to give them a voice in who should raise their children should anything unfortunate happen to them.

If you do not make your wishes clearly known in a will, it will be up to a judge to make that decision for you. There will be a trial. The judge will hear evidence from people who probably aren't speaking well of each other. Here are some things to consider about this issue through the eyes of Maria:

1. *If someone else needed to raise my kids, what parenting philosophy would I want him or her to follow?* Maria wanted her brother, Fredrico,

to raise her kids if anything happened to her or her husband. But Fredrico had odd habits and a cranky worldview that she didn't want to pass onto her children. So, she wrote down that Fredrico should teach the kids compassion, moderation, and respect for cultural differences.

2. *What values, religious and otherwise, do I want to pass along?* A self-described "lapsed Catholic," Maria nevertheless thought it was important to teach her children her heritage and the importance of community giving. She also wanted the kids to learn Spanish and make regular trips to see their *abuela* and *abuelo*.

3. *What do we want our children to know about our life story?* Maria and her husband wrote out a short family history and a family tree.

Chapter 12

Why Should I Work with Your Estate Planning Team?

If you're a do-it-yourself-er, you might be tempted to "have a go" at creating your own estate plan using tools available online. But simple, the planning process (usually) is not! You'll have to understand many technical rules and address them skillfully.

Also, recognize that when you are incapacitated or dead, you don't get a "do-over." You can't monitor the process after the fact.

Finally, appreciate the high stakes. A bad strategy can burden your family and needlessly strip thousands, tens of thousands, or even hundreds of thousands of dollars from your estate. It's not just the fees, taxes, and creditor issues, it's that your loved ones will have to clean up the mess.

Take action now.

I want to thank you for spending time with me. Hopefully, you're now (at least slightly) less confused by the why's and wherefores of estate planning and also more motivated to get to work on this critical "Quadrant 2" activity. Your future self and loved ones are counting on you.

Normally, I charge prospective clients $300.00 for a thorough discussion about their estate planning goals, but I'd like to offer you a consultation as a FREE gift. A "thank you" from me to you for taking the time to read this book and consider its ideas.

Please call my offices at **435-218-7773** to schedule this consultation now, and obtain the clarity and peace of mind that you deserve!

Take action today toward

PEACE OF MIND AND

CLARITY ABOUT YOUR FUTURE!

Call our office TODAY!
Make your appointment for a
FREE CONSULTATION
$300.00

Take CONTROL Of Your Future and Your Legacy!
Call:
435-218-7773

www.saintgeorgelaw.com/legacybook

I will share all of your options.
Your Future Awaits!

www.ingramcontent.com/pod-product-compliance
Lightning Source LLC
Chambersburg PA
CBHW071430220526
45469CB00004B/1477